WATERLOO TO WEYMOUTH

by Steam into Wessex

WATERLOO TO WEYMOUTH

by Steam into Wessex

MIKE ESAU

Ian Allan
PUBLISHING

First published 2014

ISBN 978 0 7110 3801 1

Published by Ian Allan Publishing Ltd, Hersham,
Surrey, KT12 4RG.

Printed in England.

Visit the Ian Allan Publishing website at
www.ianallanpublishing.com

Picture Credits
All photographs were taken by the author.

Front cover Photographed from the hillside
to the south of Shawford station, 'Battle of
Britain' No 34071 *601 Squadron* is on a down
train for Bournemouth. On the right of the
picture is the spire of St Mary's church in
Twyford village.

Rear cover As the sun sets beneath a stormy
sky, a rebuilt Bulleid Pacific forges north near
Wallers Ash.

Page 1 'Steam Into Wessex' – south of
Micheldever, rebuilt 'Battle of Britain' Pacific
No 34085 *501 Squadron* speeds down the 1 in
252 gradient towards Winchester with a train
for Bournemouth.

Page 2 Railtours, such as the 'South West
Suburban', run by the Locomotive Club of
Great Britain (LCGB), on 5 February 1967,
provided a colourful change from the
mundane day-to-day workings on the main
line. Rebuilt 'West Country' No 34100
Appledore has been beautifully cleaned for
the tour that it worked from Shepperton to
Twickenham – I have photographed it near
Shepperton not long after 11am. No less than
six different locomotives were used for this
tour which culminated in a run from Hampton
Court and thence up the main line to Waterloo
behind rebuilt 'Battle of Britain' No 34077.

Above Leaving Upwey & Broadwey station
the line ran along an embankment making
it an ideal location for photographing trains
leaving for Dorchester. In this broadside view
the powerful lines of BR Standard Class 4
No 75077 with its double blastpipe chimney
and substantial BR1B tender are seen to good
advantage. Happily another example of the
class, No 75079, is currently undergoing
restoration at Ropley on the Mid-Hants Railway.

INDEX OF LOCATIONS

INTRODUCTION

WITH THE 50TH ANNIVERSARY of the end of steam on the Southern Region approaching, it seemed an appropriate time to recall those far off days with a new portrait of the line in the 10 years or so up to July 1967.

In this book, I have arranged my photographs in geographical sequence from Waterloo to Weymouth and included some images from routes associated and connecting with the main line – for example the then important railway centre of Feltham between Richmond and Staines on the line to Reading, Pirbright Junction to Winchester Junction via Alton – 'Over the Alps', the attractive branches to Lymington and Swanage, and glimpses of the Didcot, Newbury and Southampton (DNS) and the Somerset & Dorset (S&D) which ran through Wessex. With only a few exceptions, none of the photographs have been published before.

Waterloo to Weymouth was destined to be Britain's last steam-operated main line, offering a chance for the enthusiast to experience the thrill of everyday high speed running whether travelling on the train or watching from the line side. This was especially true of the section between Basingstoke and Woking where speeds in excess of 100mph were recorded behind Bulleid Pacifics – a final flowering of main line steam power. The last steam-hauled trains ran on 9 July 1967.

However thanks to a change in policy, steam was allowed to run again on the line in 1992 after a gap of 25 years. Special trains now regularly operate between London and Wessex to destinations such as Bournemouth and Weymouth, worked by a variety of preserved locomotives including Nos 34046 *Braunton,* 34067 *Tangmere* and 35028 *Clan Line.* Who would have thought that not far short of 50 years since working steam fini, the melodious 'Middle C' sound of a Bulleid Pacific's whistle continues to be heard drifting across the broad acres of Surrey, Hampshire and Dorset, maintaining the traditions of days gone by.

Compared with the 1960s and in contrast with the other lines out of the capital, there has been surprisingly little visual change over the route, particularly as the continued use of the tried and tested third-rail electrification system has ensured that no intrusive overhead wire catenary obscures the view from the lineside.

Most of the principal stations are essentially unaltered, though their facilities have been modernised over the years. Waterloo has been expanded to include the International station, though this is being adapted and used for domestic services now that trains for the Continent run from St Pancras. Clapham Junction has seen improvements to some of its platforms but other distinctive stations like Surbiton, Woking and Bournemouth remain almost unchanged, though better cared for than they were in steam days.

As might be expected there is now virtually nothing left of the steam age infrastructure, and of course all the locomotive s have long gone – Nine Elms 70A (now the new Covent Garden market), Feltham (70B) (an industrial estate), Basingstoke (70D) (office buildings), Bournemouth (71B) (car park) and Weymouth (71G) (housing), though the site of Eastleigh (71A) remains in railway use as a traincare depot. Happily Eastleigh Works is still in operation albeit on a reduced scale. Also the site centered around the one-time power station at Durnsford Road between Earlsfield and Wimbledon, remains in railway use as a maintenance and stabling depot for electric stock.

Though the classic ocean liner traffic is only a memory, the Port of Southampton is still very important, the originating point for the many lengthy container trains which speed along the line to Basingstoke and on to the Midlands. How different these workings are to an 'S15' 4-6-0, or BR Standard Class 5, plodding along with a long rake of four-wheel wagons in steam days.

On the motive power front not far short of 50 different locomotive types are depicted in this book – even in the late 1950s/early 1960s when the older Adams and Drummond classes had been withdrawn, there still remained a wide variety of motive power to be photographed particularly the charismatic Drummond 'T9s' and 'M7s'. Right up to the end though, the heroes were the Southern Region enginemen and fitters whose efforts allowed the iconic Bulleid Pacifics to see main line steam out with such memorable style and panache.

Preparation of this book and researching the information for the captions has been a wonderful exercise in nostalgia and I am indebted to those who have assisted me – Roger Cruse and John Fry of the Bulleid Society for all things 'Bulleid', Roger Merry-Price for patiently answering my many queries and especially timetable and locomotive working information, Paul Blowfield who was professionally involved in the running of steam on the Waterloo–Weymouth route in the mid to late 1990s, Andrew P. M. Wright of the Swanage Railway deep in 'Wessex' country, my brother David with whom I shared many railway trips and Nick, Kevin and Alistair at Ian Allan Publishing for the opportunity to produce this book. One who is sadly not with us any more is my lifelong friend and railway enthusiast Dr Gerald Siviour, who passed away in October 2013 – we spent many enjoyable hours watching and photographing steam on the 'South Western' main line, particularly when he was in residence at Southampton University studying for his degree.

Finally and not least, my thanks are due to my wife Alison for her constructive help at all stages of the book's preparation – quite apart from reading through my captions and suggesting improvements, she provided invaluable objective and unbiased advice when I was trying to decide which pictures should be included and which not.

It simply remains for me to say that I hope you enjoy this journey down Britain's last steam main line.

Mike Esau
Richmond, Surrey
March 2014

One misty morning near Fleet, my son Richard and his teddy watch a rebuilt Bulleid Pacific making for London with a semi-fast service from Basingstoke. Though this picture has appeared in the first and second editions of my earlier book *Steam Into Wessex*, it has proved so popular that I thought it merited being placed here. In 2002 it was used by Ian Allan Publishing in connection with their celebration of 60 years in the trade.

Waterloo

Right The big flag stretched out above the Houses of Parliament seen behind the tender of rebuilt 'Battle of Britain' No 34050 *Royal Observer Corps*, shows that there is a cold easterly gale blowing. The white lights on the signal showing 'MT' (Main Through) indicate that No 34050 has the road at Waterloo, its steam and smoke blown forward in a rather spectacular way by the wind.

Below The entrance to Waterloo from York Road in the mid-1960s, the station somewhat disfigured by the shabby 'British Rail' façade facing the camera and the hoarding in front of the lion. In the background the Victory Arch built between 1919 and 1922 provides a dignified entrance to the station despite the adjacent building work.

Above The block of flats overlooking the north side of the line outside Waterloo provided a grandstand view of the comings and goings at the great terminus station. In this picture taken on 20 June 1959, the London skyline towards the City awaits the arrival of the tall buildings we are familiar with today and is still dominated by St Paul's Cathedral. In the foreground evidence remains of the heavy bomb damage this area suffered in the war. Beyond the big girder bridge, Lower Marsh basks in the hot summer sunshine, probably little changed from the late 1940s. Salisbury shed's 'King Arthur' No 30452 *Sir Meliagrance* is being used to work empty stock to Clapham Junction carriage sidings. Among the trains in the station are a Maunsell Mogul 2-6-0 and a rebuilt Bulleid Pacific as well as 4COR and 4SUB electric multiple-units.

Below Two rebuilt Bulleid Pacifics stand at the buffer stops at Waterloo on a cold wet winter evening. Despite the protection from the weather afforded by the station's overall roof, the platforms are soaked with condensation making them quite slippery for the unwary traveller. In the background some mailbags and boxes wait to be dealt with.

Right The 'country' ends of the principal main line platforms at Waterloo were popular with enthusiasts and spotters, especially after work during the evening peak when several steam arrivals and departures could be seen in quick succession. This picture featuring rebuilt 'Battle of Britain' Pacific No 34087 entering the platform with a boat train from Southampton Docks, speaks for itself – were you there?

Above Among the final duties for the 'King Arthur' class were semi-fast trains on the Waterloo-Basingstoke-Salisbury line. One of the last survivors was No 30798 *Sir Hectimere,* withdrawn in June 1962 from Salisbury shed, which had a reputation for keeping its locomotives clean. The burnished knight is resting by the buffer stops at Waterloo after arrival at 11.16am with a train from its home city.

Below Here is the busy scene at Waterloo in May 1964 with two rebuilt Bulleid Pacifics. On the left the 'Bournemouth Belle' is slowly pulling out behind a rather dirty 'Merchant Navy' No 35029 *Ellerman Lines* which is without the usual headboard. To the right No 34077 *603 Squadron* is waiting to leave on the following 12.35pm Saturdays Only train to Bournemouth. On the far left another BR Standard Class 3 No 82016 is on station empty stock duties. The 'Mind the Gap' signs are a reminder of the curved nature of some of the main line platforms at Waterloo.

Above The premier train of the day to Bournemouth was the 'Bournemouth Belle' that left Waterloo at 12.30pm with one stop at Southampton Central. This enabled the traveller to reach the seaside resort in style in return for a supplement. In 1962 for instance, this was 6s (30p) 1st Class or 4s (20p) 2nd Class (about £5.50 and £3.60 respectively at today's equivalent values). At the barrier a passenger has his ticket checked whilst in the background a BR Standard Class 3 2-6-2T waits to give the train a helping push out of the station. Note the machine on the right of the picture that dispensed paper platform tickets.

Left Against the background of Petrofina House (left) and the Shell Building (centre), BR Standard Class 4 2-6-4T No 80133 is leaving the station with a vans train. The fireman of rebuilt 'West Country' No 34009 *Lyme Regis* is climbing back to the safety of the locomotive's footplate before it works an empty stock filling-in turn to Clapham Junction carriage sidings.

Left A sailor on the platform at Waterloo, likely to be on his way to Portsmouth Harbour, watches Urie 'King Arthur' 4-6-0 No 30748 *Vivien* arriving with a semi-fast train from Basingstoke. This locomotive was withdrawn in September 1957 some years before the demise of the last 'King Arthur' of all, No 30770 *Sir Prainius* in November 1962. The 'West Country' in the background No 34094 *Morthoe,* did little better lasting only until August 1964 after less than 15 years in service. On the right in the background is a glimpse of Waterloo's distinctive concrete signalbox opened in 1936 but finally closed in 1990.

Above Rebuilt 'Merchant Navy' No 35023 *Holland-Afrika Line* is waiting to leave Waterloo with a Bournemouth line train, whilst on an adjacent platform a Standard Class 5 coasts into the station. No 35023 led a distinguished career, often used on the prestigious 'Atlantic Coast Express' and survived right to the end of steam, though sadly was not saved for preservation. The oil and grease evident on the tracks in this picture underlines the difficulty in making a clean start at Waterloo where sanding was not permitted since it might interfere with the track circuits.

Right Meanwhile another rebuilt 'Battle of Britain' No 34053 *Sir Keith Park* has been given the right away at Waterloo on the 1.30pm to Bournemouth. As the train starts its journey, Bournemouth shed fireman Les Gallon is perhaps contemplating the run ahead on this bleak winter day. In contrast to the two-hour trains, the 1.30pm was not one of the fastest of the day in the early 1960s. With several stops en route it was not due at the resort until 4.15pm.

Vauxhall

Left The block of flats from which I took the picture of No 30452 on page 9, also gave a fine view of the line towards Vauxhall. Here 'King Arthur' No 30783 *Sir Gillemere* is approaching Waterloo on 20 June 1959 with a boat train from Southampton Docks that includes a Pullman car.

Below left Those who experienced the severe winter of 1962/63 will never forget the seemingly unending days of cloud, snow and icy temperatures. In similar conditions this picture was taken a year earlier in January 1962, Shrouded by freezing fog, Salisbury based 'King Arthur' No 30796 *Sir Dodinas le Savage* moves cautiously away from Vauxhall with an up semi-fast train.

Below right With the completion of the Kent Coast electrification scheme, some of the locomotives that had been made redundant, including a few Maunsell 'L1' 4-4-0s, were transferred to the Western Section of the Southern Region. There was little work for them to do but a regular turn was the 12.42pm Saturdays Only train from Waterloo to Basingstoke which I have photographed passing Vauxhall in charge of former Dover Marine locomotive No 31753. In the background work is forging ahead on the tall office blocks that now dominate the area.

Nine Elms shed (70A)

Left Close to the exit from Nine Elms shed to the main line, rebuilt 'Merchant Navy' No 35004 *Cunard White Star,* which looks in fine condition, is about to back down to the coaling tower to refill its tender.

Left West Country' No 34041 *Wilton* is ready to move on to the turntable at the end of the yard adjacent to Brooklands Road, where the entrance to the shed was located. Nine Elms' impressive coaling tower can be seen in the background of this picture. After the shed closed in July 1967, the demolition contractor had his work cut out to remove this tough reinforced concrete structure.

Right 'Chorus Line' – there is an impressive display of motive power in the roofless part of the shed on 24 June 1964. From the camera, Maunsell 'U' class 2-6-0 No 31621, another Maunsell 2-6-0, but fitted with a BR pattern chimney and new cylinders, a rebuilt Bulleid Pacific, BR Standard Class 5 4-6-0 No 73115 *King Pellinore,* a BR Standard Class 4 4-6-0 and rebuilt and unrebuilt Bulleid Pacifics. The shed suffered badly from bombing in World War 2 and was never properly rebuilt. After closure the area it once covered disappeared under the new Covent Garden Market.

Left The incomparable atmosphere of the working steam shed is seen here at its best. Waiting for the next turn of duty inside the shed on Sunday 26 September 1965, is rebuilt 'Battle of Britain' Pacific No 34077 *603 Squadron* standing alongside BR Standard Class 3 2-6-2T No 82026.

Right The 'M7' class was long associated with the empty stock workings between Waterloo and the carriage sidings at Clapham Junction. No 30249 was one of a band of hard working city 'M7s', their duties far different from those of their relations quietly seeing out their days on some country branch line. No 30249 soldiered on until July 1963, but happily sister locomotive No 30245 was saved for the National Collection at York. Apart from the arrival of some ex GWR pannier tanks in 1959, the BR Standard Class 3 2-6-2Ts such as No 82016, seen standing beside 'West Country' No 34007 *Wadebridge*, began to take over the 'M7' workings in 1962 and lasted until the end of steam on the Southern Region.

Left Almost forgotten right at the back of the shed is 'L' No 31768, another refugee transferred from the Eastern Section. There was little work available though No 31768 was employed on Christmas parcel train duties from Waterloo in 1960. However its moment of glory came slightly earlier on 18 September 1960 when it worked the LCGB 'South Western Limited' train from Ascot to Eastleigh (see page 49).

Queen's Road

Right The island platform at Queen's Road was ideally placed for photographing rush hour trains leaving the capital, especially on sunny evenings when the sun was at just the right angle. Working an empty stock train from Clapham Junction to Waterloo formed of smartly turned out Bulleid coaches, BR Standard Class 3 No 82025 is coming under the bridge carrying the Victoria main line.

Below One of Nine Elms tough old 'M7s' No 30321 is trundling past the station with a lengthy train of empty stock bound for Clapham Junction carriage sidings. Behind the locomotive looms the bulk of Hampton's Depository that was situated adjacent to Stewarts Lane shed. No 30321 was withdrawn in September 1962.

Right Working an evening Waterloo–Bournemouth line train, rebuilt 'West Country' No 34009 *Lyme Regis* is passing Queen's Road station. Unusually the train appears to be formed of all maroon painted BR Mk 1 and ex LMS stock, possibly borrowed by the Southern Region from an inter-regional working to Bournemouth.

Clapham Junction

Above I am standing on the wide covered footbridge linking all the platforms at Clapham Junction that was an excellent vantage point for photography in steam days. Rebuilt 'Battle of Britain' No 34089 *602 Squadron* is leaning to the curve with the 5.43pm train to Salisbury, though the clock on the wall on the right of the picture appears to be showing about five past six so perhaps the train was running a little late or the clock was wrong! The footbridge is still in use but has been refurbished in recent years.

Above The celebrated heavy 3.54pm Clapham Junction–West of England milk train empties via East Putney, was sometimes double-headed for the climb through Wandsworth Town station. The train is entering Clapham Junction at the beginning of its journey behind BR Standard Class 5 No 73111 piloted by 'M7' No 30241, which will come off at Wimbledon Park. This train was something of a spotters' delight as it was sometimes worked by Bulleid light Pacifics from Exmouth Junction shed, that were uncommon east of Salisbury.

Right On a different occasion here is the 5.43pm Waterloo to Salisbury train again. The driver has eased rebuilt 'West Country' No 34026 *Yes Tor* for the 40mph speed restriction through the station, causing the safety valves to lift. The flimsy looking structure on the right leads to the subway and typifies the rather rundown condition of the station in the 1960s.

Left Between Queens Road station and Clapham Junction the line from Waterloo runs parallel to the Brighton line from Victoria. In steam days there was always the chance to glimpse interesting motive power working Oxted, Tunbridge Wells West and East Grinstead line services, or even a Newhaven boat train, perhaps in charge of one of the remaining 'H2' class Brighton Atlantics. The last of these in service, No 32424 *Beachy Head*, made its farewell run on 13 April 1958 at 10.25am from Victoria to Newhaven, seen here passing Clapham Junction in fine style at around 50mph. Although No 32424 was a significant loss to the preservation movement, a full size replica locomotive is currently under construction at Sheffield Park on the Bluebell Railway.

Right Of even earlier construction than the 'H2', a few 'T9' 4-4-0s were still enlivening the scene in the London area in the late 1950s, such as No 30719 slowly running into Clapham Junction yard with a vans train on Nine Elms 'T9' Duty 48 in 1958. No 30719 together with sister locomotive No 30338, were the last 'T9s' working in the London area and they left for a new life at Exmouth Junction shed on 17 June 1959 where No 30719 survived until March 1961.

Above A favourite subject for railway photographers was the 'Kenny Belle' service that ran during the morning and evening rush hours between Clapham Junction and Kensington Olympia. Although it was primarily for Post Office workers, anyone could buy a ticket to travel on the trains. At the time I took this photograph, the services were worked by 'H' class 0-4-4Ts from Stewarts Lane shed. No 31542 is waiting to leave the spacious station at Olympia for Clapham Junction on 17 August 1962. A little later at Clapham Junction, the 'H' is arriving on the far 'South Western' side of the station

Right Rebuilt 'Merchant Navy' No 35027 *Port Line* has just passed Clapham Junction in January 1965 with the down 'Bournemouth Belle'. Of note are the lines of washing, the absence of graffiti and the beautifully kept condition of the permanent way.

Earlsfield

Below Leaving Clapham Junction, the Bournemouth line enters Clapham cutting that extends almost all the way to Earlsfield, 5½ miles from Waterloo. On a cold but sunny winter morning, a BR Standard Class 5 4-6-0 is heading west towards Earlsfield.

Above In complete contrast to the previous picture, three trains pass in the cutting near Earlsfield one summer afternoon – a BR Standard Class 4 4-6-0 is running light engine on the down local line, whilst a 4COR EMU is about to pass an up Bournemouth train headed by a rebuilt Bulleid Pacific. Note how clear the embankment sides are of trees compared to now.

Above Rebuilt 'Battle of Britain' No 34071 *601 Squadron* is hurrying past Durnsford Road power station and depot with the summer Saturday 11.15am Waterloo to West of England train. Among the electric units in the depot is 4COR No 3103 primarily used on fast services to Portsmouth. The power station and depot were brought into use by the LSWR in 1915 to provide electricity and maintenance facilities for its new electric services. A familiar sight to travellers was LSWR Bo-Bo electric locomotive No DS74, used for moving coal wagons there for many years until it was scrapped in July 1965. After Durnsford Road was closed in the mid-1960s, the maintenance depot was enlarged to cover the site and continues to be a busy and important facility.

Wimbledon

Left Trying to identify this freight train has proved to be rather difficult. The hefty 'H16' 4-6-2Ts were regular visitors to Wimbledon where they could be seen in the west yard. Carrying 'Spl' (Special) on one of the three discs of its headcode, Feltham shed's No 30516 is passing the station in 1958 on the up main line with a train which is likely to be destined for Nine Elms goods depot.

Left The path which runs alongside the line for some distance to the west of Wimbledon gives a fine view of the trains, though this has been spoilt in recent years by the replacement of the original iron railings by high security fencing. A 4SUB electric multiple-unit is passing the one time milk delivery platform close to the station, as No 34089 *602 Squadron* emerges into the evening sunshine with the 5.43pm train from Waterloo to Salisbury. In the background the line to West Croydon curves away towards Merton Park.

Raynes Park to Berrylands

Left On 28 March 1965, soon after Raynes Park station, 'Merchant Navy' No 35007 *Aberdeen Commonwealth* on the down 'Bournemouth Belle' is passing the site of Carters Tested Seeds which was in the process of being redeveloped for housing.

Left In the up direction seen from the bridge carrying the A3 road over the railway, BR Standard Class 3 2-6-2T No 82028 is heading into London on the same date with a train of vans and empty coaching stock.

Right The wide footbridge just to the east of New Malden station gave an excellent view of the trains (and indeed still does). Due to Sunday bridge renewal work at the station in the summer of 1959, rebuilt 'Merchant Navy' No 35024 *East Asiatic Company* has been routed on to the up local line with a train from Bournemouth. An interesting selection of stock, including two large cranes and a wagon carrying new bridge girders, is parked on the down fast line headed by what looks like a Maunsell Mogul.

Right In August 1962 'Lord Nelson' No 30861 *Lord Anson* is passing Berrylands station on the goods train that left Nine Elms depot around 8pm for Basingstoke and Southampton. On this summer evening the locomotive is displaying a lamp rather than a disc as it will probably be dark by the time the train reaches Basingstoke. The station, dating from the early 1930s, was primarily built to serve the surrounding new housing estates. A notable feature was the wooden platforms that must have been very hazardous in wet or frosty weather.

Right Between Berrylands and Surbiton the line enters a deep cutting crossed by King Charles Road on a narrow steel bridge which was a good vantage point to photograph the passing trains. This down Bournemouth service is hauled by 'Lord Nelson' No 30864 *Sir Martin Frobisher*.

Left BR Standard Class 5 No 73171 had the distinction of being the last one built of this large class of 172 locomotives. It was sent new to York in May 1957, transferred to the Southern Region in 1963 and ended its days at Eastleigh, from where it was withdrawn in October 1966 after an incredibly short life of just over nine years. Here it is working a down train at Berrylands and about to pass a '76000' class 2-6-0 on a train from Basingstoke.

Surbiton and Thames Ditton

Left Here is the 8.35am train from Waterloo to Bournemouth and Weymouth that called at Surbiton at 8.53am to pick up only. In earlier times it was a regular turn for a 'Lord Nelson', but towards the end of steam in the winter of 1966/67, it is being worked by a sadly neglected looking rebuilt 'Merchant Navy' No 35023 which is without its *Holland-Afrika Line* nameplates. Surbiton station's distinctive clock tower can be seen on the left in the background. .

Right On 2 and 16 December 1962 the RCTS and SLS ran two farewell specials for the Beattie Well Tanks which for so many years had worked down in Wadebridge on the Wenford Bridge branch. 16 December was a glorious day and I seem to be alone on the platform at Thames Ditton station to photograph the special headed by Nos 30585 and 30587 as it makes for Hampton Court.

34

Esher to Walton-on-Thames

Above The up lines are closed at Esher station to allow bridge repairs to take place on the hot Sunday of 15 May 1955. I expect the crew of '700' class 0-6-0 No 30325 from Guildford shed will be enjoying a comparatively quiet time in charge of this engineer's train.

Right Rebuilt 'Merchant Navy' No 35030 *Elder Dempster Lines* passes the impressively tall down fast line signal at Esher on a train for Bournemouth.

Below Working the 2.54pm Waterloo to Basingstoke train, 'King Arthur' No 30451 *Sir Lamorak* is passing Esher station for Sandown Park racecourse on 24 February 1962. Withdrawn in June 1962, No 30451 was the last of the 1925 Eastleigh-built 'King Arthurs' in service.

Right Frost is still coating the sleepers as 'West Country' No 34102 *Lapford* which is probably travelling at around 80 mph, speeds towards Esher station with a lightweight train from Salisbury. No 34102 was a candidate for preservation, however No 34023 *Blackmore Vale* was chosen instead.

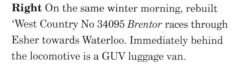

Right On the same winter morning, rebuilt 'West Country No 34095 *Brentor* races through Esher towards Waterloo. Immediately behind the locomotive is a GUV luggage van.

Above Rebuilt 'Merchant Navy' No 35008 *Orient* Line is passing the upper quadrant signals between Walton-on-Thames and Weybridge. The Southern Region ran two special trains to mark the end of steam on the Bournemouth line on 2 July 1967. No 35008, which has had its nameplates reinstated, is on the first of these trains which left Waterloo at 9.55am for the run to Bournemouth and Weymouth.

Above On 16 April 1966 the RCTS organised a special train from Waterloo to the Longmoor Military Railway. Among the last of the Maunsell Mogul 2-6-0s in service were 'N' No 31411 and 'U' No 31639 that worked the outward leg as far as Woking. Here they are passing Weybridge.

Left Rebuilt 'Battle of Britain' No 34060 *25 Squadron* is passing the electricity sub station at Weybridge with a down Bournemouth line train. To the left of the picture is the line to Addlestone and Virginia Water.

Left The LCGB special 'The A2 Commemorative Rail Tour' run on 14 August 1966 had its problems. LNER 'A2' Pacific No 60532 *Blue Peter* brought specially from Scotland, was the star of the show but unfortunately dogged by poor steaming on its run down to Exeter. However it appears to be going quite well as it passes Walton-on-Thames on the down slow line, not long after the beginning of its journey scheduled at 9.52am from Waterloo. BR 'Britannia' class No 70004 *William Shakespeare* worked the train back from Westbury to Waterloo.

Feltham shed (70B) and yard

Above left Feltham shed (70B) provided motive power for some of the freight services on the main lines to Bournemouth and the West of England. It was located adjacent to the huge marshalling yard opened by the LSWR during World War 1 and closed on 6 January 1969. The shed was of the 'through' variety being open at both ends – these photographs give some idea of the atmosphere of this large depot. On Saturday 13 February 1965, a BR Standard Class 2-6-0 and 2-6-4T No 80154 are filling the air inside the shed with acrid smoke as they await their next turns of duty. No 80154 was notable as not only being the last of the class to be built, but also the last locomotive to be constructed at Brighton Works

Above right Just inside the end of the shed on the same day, I have been able to take a powerful picture from a low angle of Standard Class 5 No 73084 *Tintagel*. The light from outside is nicely picking out the oil and grime on the workaday looking locomotive

Above In April 1959 at the west end of the yard, not far from Feltham station, tough old No 30567 is engaged on shunting duties. As late as March 1957 sister locomotive No 30575 was given a general overhaul in Eastleigh Works and No 30567 was repaired and repainted there in May of the same year.

Right Two classes of locomotive that were synonymous with Feltham were the Adams '0395' class and the much later Bulleid 'Q1' 0-6-0. No 30567 was built in 1883 and destined to be the last of the class in service, not being withdrawn until September 1959. The 'Q1' was a versatile and useful class of locomotive, but No 33006 was withdrawn at the beginning of 1966 after a life of only 24 years. Glimpsed on the far right of the picture is the cab of 'G16' 4-8-0T No 30493 which was mainly used in the hump yard at Feltham.

Feltham to West Byfleet

Above The spire of St Catherine's church dominates the scene to the right of the picture as BR Standard Class 5 No 73113 gets a freight train from Feltham yard on the move. The locomotive is carrying the West of England headcode, so at Virginia Water the train should turn off towards Addlestone and Weybridge, joining the main line via the spur to Byfleet and New Haw.

Top right Given the uncertainty of the timings for freight workings, I have been fortunate to photograph this Feltham-bound train near Ashford behind 'U' 2-6-0 No 31809.

The greenhouses on the right of the picture emphasise the importance of market gardening in this flat and fertile Thames Valley area.

Bottom right At West Byfleet station the driver of BR Standard Class 5 No 73022 has shut off steam ready for a stop at Woking another three miles or so further on. Note the '6 8 12' marker at the end of the platforms to guide the driver of electric-units of these coach lengths, where to stop. There is much other period detail to see here such as the flower beds, the station name on its ornate lamp standard, the signals and the permanent way hut.

Woking to Pirbright

Below On the penultimate day of steam working on the Southern Region, 8 July 1967, rebuilt 'Merchant Navy' No 35023 *Holland-Afrika Line* pulls away from Woking after stopping with the last up Channel Islands boat train. In the siding on the down side of the line, a BR Standard 2-6-4T, carrying the West of England line headcode, is probably waiting to run light engine to Salisbury shed where it will await disposal for scrap.

Left Crossing over from the up slow line to the fast, rebuilt 'Battle of Britain' No 34053 *Sir Keith Park* coasts into Woking station past the distinctive Southern Railway built signalbox. No 34053, another of the lucky 'Barry Band of Bulleid Brothers', escaped from the scrap yard to start a new life in preservation. The locomotive has now been restored to working order and is currently based on the Severn Valley Railway.

Right Woking shares the same Southern Railway Art Deco style of architecture as Surbiton as can be seen in this picture. Rebuilt 'Battle of Britain' No 34056 *Croydon* is on a stopping service to Basingstoke, whilst beside it Class 42 'Warship' diesel-hydraulic No D817 *Foxhound* is working a West of England train. No D817 was in service for little longer than the Bulleid Pacific being withdrawn in October 1971.

Left 'On this frosty winter morning, West Country' No 34006 *Bude* is standing in the up siding as a westbound service in charge of BR Standard Class 5 No 73089 gets its train away towards Basingstoke.

Above Clutching his teddy, my two year old son Richard, who came with me on many trips into Wessex, watches rebuilt 'Merchant Navy' No 35012 *United States Line* making a steamy departure from Woking with a down West of England train.

Left Bound for the Farnham and Alton line, 'N' class 2-6-0 No 31816 leaves the down local line platform with a Christmas parcels train. The locomotive was one of the last of its class in service being withdrawn in January 1966.

Right In the days when the lineside was generally rather clearer of bushes and trees than now, it was possible to take pictures such as this near Pirbright. Rebuilt 'Merchant Navy' No 35008 *Orient Line* working a down train, makes an attractive sight passing a pond and the pine trees that abound in this area.

Below The Basingstoke Canal runs adjacent to the main line in the Brookwood area and is seen here at Brookwood locks to the west of the station and close to Pirbright Camp. On the high embankment above the canal, a rebuilt Bulleid Pacific is catching the evening sun as it heads towards Basingstoke.

Above At the end of the long climb from Woking in the vicinity of milepost 31, 'S15' No 30824 is plodding along the down local line with this lengthy freight for Basingstoke in March 1964. The line here was a popular location for railway photographers especially for westbound trains since there was plenty of room to stand back from the lineside.

Bentley to Alresford

Left An alternative route from Waterloo into Hampshire was from Pirbright Junction to Winchester Junction via Farnham, or 'Over the Alps' as it was popularly known due to the steep climbs in both directions west of Alton. Bentley was the main line station for the Bordon branch, which closed to passengers on 16 September 1957. On this misty morning shortly before services ceased, 'M7' No 30027 from Guildford shed is pulling out of the up platform at Bentley with the branch train consisting of a Urie 'Ironclad' push and pull set.

Above The tour also took in the branch to Bordon, hauled on both Sundays by 'U' No 31639 which has just passed Kingsley Halt on a snowy 16 January.

Above This special train, 'The S15 Commemorative Rail Tour', ran to Eastleigh via Alton on two consecutive Sundays, 9 and 16 January 1966, hauled by Feltham shed's nicely turned out 'S15' No 30837. On the second Sunday the 'S15' was assisted from Alton to Eastleigh by 'U' 2-6-0 No 31639. This train is seen here between Bentley and Alton.

Above The Christmas period, especially in the late 1950s and early 1960s, often produced interesting parcels trains run to cope with the large amount of extra mail. Here is Guildford shed's 'M7' No 30132 on an outing to the country with such a working. It has paused at a misty Farnham before continuing its journey west to Alton on 16 December 1961.

Above Hauling a two-coach push and pull set composed of ex-LSWR coaches on an Alton to Eastleigh service on 29 August 1957, 'M7' No 30125 makes a delightful sight as it waits at Alresford station to pass an up train which can be seen in the adjacent platform The surroundings look virtually the same today thanks to the efforts of the Mid-Hants Railway.

Right On 18 September 1960, 'L' class 4-4-0 No 31768, was used on this LCGB railtour, 'The South Western Limited'. In glorious weather, the splendidly turned out 'L', which took the train over at Ascot, is climbing the bank between Alton and Medstead & Four Marks bound for Eastleigh.

Brookwood to Basingstoke

Left Showing signs of scorching on the smokebox door, a rather neglected looking rebuilt 'Merchant Navy' No 35011 *General Steam Navigation* is working hard through Brookwood station with a down Bournemouth line train.

Above Rebuilt 'Merchant Navy' No 35027 *Port Line* has just crossed over the Guildford to Reading and Ash Vale to Frimley lines east of Farnborough with the up 'Bournemouth Belle' passing here around about 6pm. The distinctive dome of the Benedictine St Michael's Abbey can be seen on the hillside in the far distance behind the train.

Left In steam days Winchfield was a quiet station in a spacious rural setting well liked by photographers. Here rebuilt 'Battle of Britain' Pacific No 34077 *603 Squadron* is running through with the down 'Bournemouth Belle' on 30 May 1964.

Left 'West Country' No 34091 *Weymouth* is about to pass the site of Bramshot Halt on 6 June 1964 with an up semi-fast train from Salisbury. Looking very different from its 1950s heyday years working 'Golden Arrow' duties, the crinkled state of the locomotive's casing suggests that the cladding underneath has become soaked with oil and caught fire on some occasion. No 34091 was a fairly early withdrawal going for scrap not long afterwards in September 1964.

Right As recorded by pictures earlier in the book, some of the locomotives from the South Eastern Division were transferred to Western Division sheds after the implementation of the Kent Coast Electrification scheme. Far removed from previous regular use on heavy summer Saturday trains from Victoria to the Kent Coast, 'U1' 2-6-0 No 31902 is finding useful employment with a semi-fast train from Waterloo to Salisbury seen near Fleet on 17 June 1961.

Left High summer near Winchfield – rebuilt 'Merchant Navy' No 35027 *Port Line* passes a field of buttercups with a down Bournemouth line train.

Basingstoke to Reading line

Above On a hot summer Saturday 'West Country' No 34023 *Blackmore Vale* has just left Basingstoke with a train for Oxford and the north. Note the sign 'Catch Points 527 Yards' protecting the approach to the station and the main line.

Left The bright yellow flowers of a Laburnum tree and an attractive old platform gas lamp set off this picture of rebuilt 'Merchant Navy' No 35026 *Lamport & Holt Line* which is passing Winchfield station with a down Bournemouth line train.

Above The inter-regional trains provided the chance to see coaches from 'the big four' running over the Southern Region, such as these ex works Gresley vehicles at the front of a summer Saturday train, which is heading south near Silchester in charge of rebuilt 'West Country' No 34044 *Woolacombe*.

Below The Bournemouth to Manchester 'Pines Express', scheduled to depart from Basingstoke at 11.23pm on a Saturday, is about to leave watched by two smartly dressed passengers.

Above Whilst the best locomotives were generally kept for main line work on the Waterloo line, Bournemouth shed has released its smartly turned out rebuilt 'Merchant Navy' No 35027 *Port Line* for the 'Pines Express', now rerouted away from the Somerset & Dorset line. No 35027 having just left Basingstoke, will work the train as far as Oxford via the spur at Reading West and Didcot.

Left Western Region locomotives were a common sight on summer Saturday inter-regional trains to the Southern. Carrying reporting number V95, 'Modified Hall' No 7905 *Fowey Hall* is bustling north near Bramley with a return working.

Basingstoke

Right Before the arrival of more modern types, the Urie 'King Arthurs' were the regular motive power for the inter-regional services between Basingstoke and Oxford. One of these locomotives No 30751 *Etarre* is standing by the neatly constructed coal stack at its home shed Basingstoke, on 14 June 1956. It was withdrawn a year later in June 1957.

Below The footpath leading to Basingstoke shed gives a good view of the yard where BR Standard Class 5 No 73092 and rebuilt 'West Country' No 34024 await their next turns of duty. In the background on the main line, a Crompton diesel-electric is arriving with a vans train.

Right Rebuilt 'Merchant Navy' No 35012 *United States Line* has only run 48 miles from Waterloo with this train for the Salisbury line, but already its tender needs topping up at Basingstoke, emphasising the labour intensive nature of steam working. The driver is opening the stop-cock whilst his fireman, Peter Smerdon, waits patiently for the water to start flowing

Left A good crowd of enthusiasts has gathered at the west end of the station to watch the free steam age show. A down train is leaving whilst rebuilt 'West Country' No 34008 *Padstow* is arriving with a train for the Reading and Oxford line. To the right of No 34008 is Basingstoke shed.

Above Some young spotters watch Peter Smerdon, the fireman of rebuilt 'Merchant Navy' No 35012 *United States Line,* as he looks out for the 'right away' to depart for the west.

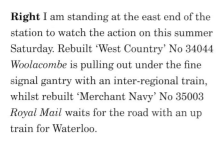

Right I am standing at the east end of the station to watch the action on this summer Saturday. Rebuilt 'West Country' No 34044 *Woolacombe* is pulling out under the fine signal gantry with an inter-regional train, whilst rebuilt 'Merchant Navy' No 35003 *Royal Mail* waits for the road with an up train for Waterloo.

Worting Junction to Oakley

Left Two miles after leaving Basingstoke and some 50 miles from Waterloo, Worting Junction marks the point where the Bournemouth and Salisbury lines part company by way of Battledown flyover. The signals are set for the Southampton line as rebuilt 'West Country' No 34026 *Yes Tor* with the down 'Bournemouth Belle', passes the railway cottages adjacent to the junction.

Below Rebuilt 'West Country' No 34036 *Westward Ho* has just crossed Battledown flyover with a through Swanage to Waterloo train, which has been routed via the Ringwood loop.

Above At Worting Junction BR Standard Class 4 No 76019 is signalled for the Salisbury line with a down train of coal empties. Nowadays new housing estates have swallowed the farmland that can be seen in this photograph and extend almost up to the railway at this point.

Right Rebuilt 'Merchant Navy' No 35004 *Cunard White Star* is about to go under the up Bournemouth line at Battledown with a train for Salisbury and the West of England.

Below left On 26 March 1966, the A4 locomotive Preservation Society ran a special train from Waterloo to Weymouth and back via Yeovil and Salisbury, anticipating present day steam workings. A4 No 60024 *Kingfisher* was rostered for this special that is seen approaching Oakley on the return run. Oakley station closed to passengers on 17 June 1963.

Below right Rebuilt 'Battle of Britain' No 34089 *602 Squadron* is passing an upper quadrant signal near Oakley with a down vans train bound for Salisbury. The track and embankments look splendidly maintained.

Battledown to Winchester

Right Passing Battledown, Stanier Class 5 No 45493, from Banbury shed, is working the York to Poole through service that was due off Basingstoke around 4.30pm. A 'regular' for this train, the Class 5 was recorded to have been 'borrowed' by Bournemouth shed for use on a working to Waterloo – the train was diverted via Alresford and Alton due to engineering work on the main line.

Below 'Schools' 4-4-0 No 30918 *Hurstpierpoint*, is approaching Battledown flyover on 17 June 1961 with a summer Saturday boat train from Lymington. Smaller locomotives had to be used on these trains because of the restricted length of the turntable at Brockenhurst.

Right I was very keen to try to get a photo of a train in the short gap between Popham No 1 and No 2 tunnels. Fortunately a helpful track ganger took me through the shorter Popham No 2 tunnel so I could obtain this shot of BR Standard Class 5 No 73085 *Melisande* on an up train.

Below The up and down platforms at Micheldever station were separated by a low grassy embankment, which can be seen in this photograph of rebuilt 'West Country' No 34013 *Okehampton* on a train from Bournemouth.

Right A present day preservationist's dream selection of rolling stock can be seen in the sidings at Micheldever. The site had its origins from work carried out in 1943 by the Southern Railway to construct an Ordnance Emergency Depot including a 2,000ft long handling shed which can be seen in this picture, by now used for berthing rolling stock. On this cold but sunny winter morning, a rebuilt Bulleid Pacific is pulling away from the station towards the two Popham tunnels (firstly Popham No 2 at 199 yards and secondly Popham No 1 at 265 yards) that take the line under the A303 road.

Left In steam days when the lineside was kept well trimmed, it was possible to take some striking silhouette pictures in the evening of trains labouring up the gradient from Winchester towards Micheldever. Set against a dramatic sky, BR Standard Class 5 4-6-0 No 73029 has just pulled out of the loop at Wallers Ash with an up train of Presflo bulk cement wagons.

Below The 'Q1' class 0-6-0s were not an everyday sight on the main line but here is No 33027 ambling downhill near Winchester Junction with a freight train probably bound for Eastleigh. No 33027 was one of the last two 'Q1s' in service being withdrawn in January 1966.

Left The Didcot, Newbury & Southampton (DNS) line passed under the South Western main line close to Winchester Junction. The diminutive figure of my son is on the bare DNS trackbed near Kings Worthy watching rebuilt 'Battle of Britain' No 34052 as it heads north on an engineers train. This section of the DNS closed to passenger traffic in 1960 and to freight four years later.

Below An attempt has been made to re-cover the roof of this rather decrepit but picturesque permanent way hut near Winchester Junction. Rebuilt 'Merchant Navy' No 35003 *Royal Mail* has steam to spare as it races past down the gradient towards the cathedral city.

Above The sun is lighting up the autumn colours near Steventon on this clear cold morning as rebuilt 'Merchant Navy' No 35027 *Port Line* works hard towards Worting Junction with the 9.13am train from Bournemouth West to Waterloo.

Above Rebuilt 'West Country' No 34004 *Yeovil* has just passed Winchester Junction signalbox, which can just be seen behind the first Pullman car, with the up 'Bournemouth Belle'. The train was scheduled to leave Southampton Central at 5.15pm, so by the time the train reached this point some 15 miles further on, the sun was in an ideal position for photography early on this summer evening.

Winchester to Shawford

Left At Winchester a road bridge gave a good view of the station from the south. Rebuilt 'Merchant Navy' No 35014 *Nederland Line* is coasting down the gradient with the 'Bournemouth Belle' and will shortly make its first stop at Southampton Central where it is due just before 2pm.

Below The hillside at Otterbourne near Shawford provided a good vantage point from which to photograph the main line running alongside the river Itchen that can be seen behind the locomotive. The driver of rebuilt 'Battle of Britain' No 34071 *601 Squadron* has shut off steam probably in anticipation for a stop at Eastleigh.

Above Some two miles south of Winchester station, the single track DNS joined the South Western main line at Shawford Junction where this picture has been taken. Rebuilt 'Merchant Navy' No 35008 *Orient Line* is passing the junction signalbox with a down train.

Right A glimpse of the picturesque DNS line that made its way north over the Wessex downland to Newbury. In charge of a train from Southampton Terminus, 'T9' No 30313, hauling three Western Region coaches, has paused at the neatly kept Whitchurch Town station.

Above Seen from inside Shawford Junction signalbox, BR Standard Class 5 No 73081 *Excalibur* is heading north with a lengthy vans train.

Lines to Fareham

Right The elegant 'T9' class was long associated with Eastleigh where they were a familiar sight for many years. No 30732 is clattering over the crossover from the Romsey direction to join the main line with a train from Andover Junction.

Left Class T9 No 30117 leaves Netley station with a typical 1950s local train on the Salisbury to Portsmouth & Southsea line. The journey time via Romsey and Southampton would be around 1½ hours. No 30117 was one of the last of the 'T9' class working from Eastleigh shed being withdrawn in July 1961. The spur line to the Royal Victoria Military Hospital Railway is on the left of the picture.

Right No 4472 *Flying Scotsman* worked the 'Scotsman Goes South' railtour from Brighton to Eastleigh on 17 September 1966. The train continued to Salisbury and back hauled by two BR Standard Class 4 2-6-4Ts. The return from Eastleigh to Victoria was worked by this famous Pacific via the coast-line and Preston Park. In lovely evening light it is seen here between Eastleigh and Fareham.

Above Botley, one-time junction for the Bishop's Waltham branch, was the first station out of Eastleigh on the Fareham line in steam days. 'U' class 2-6-0 No 31808 waits impatiently to leave the station with a train for the Romsey line.

Right To provide Eastleigh shed with modern motive power for its various duties, a number of new British Railways Standard Class 4 2-6-0s were allocated there in 1952/53. One of these locomotives, No 76017, is near Knowle Halt on the approach to Fareham with a train for Portsmouth & Southsea. Happily this locomotive has been saved and at the time of writing is undergoing overhaul at Ropley on the Mid-Hants Railway.

Eastleigh

Right The bright green livery of No 4472 *Flying Scotsman* stands out amid the grime of Eastleigh shed where it is being serviced during the course of the 'Scotsman Goes South' railtour. I was curious to know the function of the signal mounted high on the wall of the shed building and was told it was used to test enginemen's eyesight. Hopefully there is now a more scientific way of doing this!

Left You could never be sure what might be hidden away in some remote corner of a locomotive shed or works. 'Remembrance' class 4-6-0 No 32327 *Trevithick* has perhaps almost been forgotten about at Eastleigh Works on Thursday 14 June 1956. The frames and wheels in front of it once belonged to a 'USA' 0-6-0T. When working the 7.54pm train from Waterloo to Basingstoke on 23 December 1955, No 32327 was involved in an accident just to the east of Woking station when it ran into the rear of the 7.50pm Waterloo to Portsmouth Harbour electric train. Fortunately there were no serious casualties. The locomotive was eventually cut up later in 1956.

Right In sparkling lined black livery, ex-works 'Schools' No 30925 *Cheltenham* is admired by two railwaymen as it stands by the coaling stage at Eastleigh shed on 14 June 1956, after having worked a boat train to Southampton Docks.

Left Another ex-works locomotive at Eastleigh is 'G16' 4-8-0T No 30492 which is waiting to return to Feltham shed on Tuesday 1 January 1957. Behind it is Bournemouth shed's 'M7' No 30058 and on the right a Urie 'S15'.

Right A fabulous line of locomotives at Eastleigh shed on Saturday 3 November 1962 - from the right – 'M7' No 30029, preserved 'T9' No 120, 'O2' No 30199, 'B4' 0-4-0T, 'Terrier' 0-6-0T, Urie 'S15', 'Q' 0-6-0, two 'Well Tanks' Nos 30585/30587 from Wadebridge, and an 'E6' 0-6-2T.

Left On Sunday 30 April 1961 'Lord Nelson' No 30856 *Lord St Vincent* worked the LCGB 'The Solent Limited' railtour from Waterloo to Portsmouth Harbour. No 30856 has just passed Petersfield and is tackling the 1 in 100 climb to Buriton tunnel.

Left Later on, in charge of 'T9' No 30117, 'The Solent Limited' reached Southampton Central for a tour of the docks behind 'USA' No 30073. Continuing to Eastleigh on what had turned into a miserable wet afternoon, the 'USA' is arriving at the station.

Eastleigh to Southampton

Above Turning left out of Eastleigh station, which can be seen in the distance, a short walk parallel to the railway soon brings you to Campbell Road that crosses over the main line adjacent to the entrance to the works. I am standing on the bridge to photograph 'West Country' No 34019 *Bideford* coasting past with a down train. The tracks into the shed are to the right of the locomotive and in the distance, the line to Fareham.

Above Swaythling station is located between the modern Southampton Airport Parkway and St Denys. Rebuilt 'West Country' No 34040 *Crewkerne* is passing Swaythling's attractive signalbox with an up train. There appears to be plenty of room beside the box for railwaymen's allotments.

Above Flanked by Bevois Park marshalling yard on the right and the wide expanse of the river Itchen on the left as it nears the Solent, BR Standard Class 5 No 73169 is approaching St Denys with a train for Waterloo. The fine signal gantry controls the junction at St Denys with the line to Fareham and Portsmouth.

Right Two BR Standard Class 4s are meeting by the impressive signal gantry at St Denys station. No 76008 is on what is likely to be a Cardiff to Portsmouth through service which includes some Western Region Hawksworth coaches in its formation, whilst sister locomotive No 76067 is ready to proceed towards Southampton.

Above With the substantial bulk of the South Western Hotel in the background, 'T9' No 30707 is waiting to leave the Terminus station with a local train for Bournemouth. Even at the time of this 1958 photograph, it is clear that the facilities of this large station were very under utilized.

Right Between Northam and Southampton Central station the line is hemmed in on both sides by walls and buildings. 'West Country' No 34002 *Salisbury* is approaching the camera with an up train, and about to pass a Western Region cross-country unit from Portsmouth to Bristol and Cardiff. The two cars on the right are I believe an early postwar Jaguar and a Morris 1000 Traveller.

Left Southampton Terminus station, adjacent to the docks, closed on 5 September 1966. It was the starting point for trains to several destinations such as Salisbury, Alton and the DNS line. Part of the South Western hotel can be seen on the far right of the picture and beyond it the cranes in the docks and the funnel of a Cunarder liner. BR Standard Class 4 No 76053 is pulling out with a train of empty stock, whilst behind it on the far side of the station is what looks like an Ivatt 2-6-2T.

Left The angle of the low winter sun on this cold afternoon helps to contrast the clean condition of the Bulleid coaches with the filthy state of BR Standard Class 4 No 75076, which is entering Southampton Central station with an up train. Prominent on the platform to the left are the unmistakable outlines of the Southern Railway designed platform lights.

Right Shortly after leaving Southampton Central station, rebuilt 'Merchant Navy' No 35010 *Blue Star* is about enter the 528 yards long Southampton tunnel, which takes the line under the Civic Centre. The grassed area above the tunnel provides an excellent vantage point for these enthusiasts. Behind the train is the station's distinctive clock tower now long demolished.

Above Being the principal destination between Waterloo and Bournemouth, Southampton was a popular place to watch the various workings on the main line. At the Central station a good crowd of enthusiasts has gathered at the end of the down platform to watch rebuilt 'West Country' No 34040 *Crewkerne* pulling away with a train for Bournemouth.

Right Inter-regional trains regularly brought variety to the usual procession of Bulleid Pacifics such as 'Black 5' No 44860 from 2D Banbury shed, which is making a smoky departure from Southampton Central with the York to Poole service.

Facing page 'Rebuilt Merchant Navy' No 35026 *Lamport & Holt Line* has just left Southampton Central for Bournemouth. White conductor rail insulators by the track indicate that preparations for electrification of the line are under way.

Southampton to Brockenhurst

Left Rebuilt 'West Country' Pacific No 34101 *Hartland*, which I have photographed passing Millbrook goods yard on Saturday 3 November 1962, is working an inter-regional train from Brighton. It will shortly turn off the main line at Redbridge station to head towards Romsey and Salisbury. On withdrawal No 34101 was sold to Woodhams Bros at Barry, but subsequently saved. It is currently under major overhaul at the North York Moors Railway.

Above Southern Region steam on the Bournemouth line at its best - hauling a smart rake of coaches including a Bulleid open 2nd behind the locomotive, splendidly turned out rebuilt 'Battle of Britain' Pacific No 34077 *603 Squadron* passes Millbrook station en route to Bournemouth, on the same day I photographed No 34101.

Right With the characteristic throaty roar of steam from its safety valves, Salisbury shed's nicely cleaned 'T9' No 30702 is running into Romsey station in 1958 with a train from Salisbury to Portsmouth & Southsea, a journey that will take the best part of 1½ hours. There is an ex LMS van behind the locomotive followed by a three-coach Bulleid set, all painted in carmine and cream livery.

Left Further down the line towards Southampton at Nursling, BR Standard Class 4 No 76005 is passing the rather run down looking station with a train from the Western Region. The station closed in September 1957.

Left Many special trains were run as the end of steam approached like the 'Hants & Dorset Branch Flyer' on 25 March 1967. 'USA' No 30064, generally used for shunting in Southampton Docks, is returning to Totton after a trip down the Fawley branch. BR Standard tank No 80151 then took over the train for next leg of the tour to Lymington Pier.

Left Fine weather often seemed to accompany LCGB tours such as 'The South Western Limited' on 18 September 1960. After photographing the train on the Alton to Winchester line (page 49), I was able to see it again approaching Marchwood station behind 'H16' No 30516 which worked the train from Eastleigh to Fawley and back to Totton. There 'King Arthur' No 30782 *Sir Brian* took over for the run to Broadstone via the Ringwood loop.

Left Lyndhurst Road station (since renamed 'Ashurst [New Forest]') was originally so called because of its situation some distance from the town it purported to serve and is in fact is nearer the village of Ashurst. In 1966 and 1967 leading up to the end of steam on the Southern Region, a few railtours were run using 'A4' class locomotives such as this one by the 'A4 Preservation Society' on 26 March 1966 with No 60024 *Kingfisher*. On its way to Bournemouth and Weymouth, the 'A4' sweeps round the curve through the station.

Below I then moved back along the platform to photograph rebuilt 'West Country' No 34037 *Clovelly* about to pass under the rather decrepit looking footbridge with a down train.

Right In the opposite direction, rebuilt 'West Country' No 34018 *Axminster* is passing the station with the up 'Bournemouth Belle' which was due through around 5pm. This picture gives a good impression of the station's rural New Forest location

Right Pleasantly set in the New Forest, mid-way between Lyndhurst and the village of Beaulieu, Beaulieu Road station has now long lost its attractive platform awnings. On this spring day of blustery showers, BR Standard Class 4 No 76016 is arriving at the station with a stopping train for Bournemouth.

Brockenhurst and the Lymington branch

Left Towards the end of their career the 'King Arthur' class were frequently used on the inter-regional trains between Poole, Bournemouth and Oxford via Basingstoke. In the summer of 1958, No 30780 *Sir Persant* from Bournemouth shed is pulling away from Brockenhurst station up the 1 in 176 gradient towards Lymington Junction with a train formed of Maunsell stock that it will have taken over at Oxford.

Left BR Standard Class 4 tank No 80019 is simmering in the bay platform at Brockenhurst with a train for Lymington Pier. No 80019 was allocated new to the Southern Region in 1951 and finished its days at Bournemouth shed from where it was withdrawn in March 1967.

Right This polished and well cared for 'To Call Porters' button at Brockenhurst station was something of a relic from earlier times – the porters' barrows on the right stand ready to carry travelers' luggage.

Right I came across these three redundant station signs propped up against the wall at Brockenhurst station, presumably awaiting disposal. I am told that this little collection of signs might be worth in excess of £3,000 these days.

Right To the east of Brockenhurst in typical New Forest surroundings, 'Schools' 4-4-0 No 30934 *St Lawrence,* carrying the distinctive Waterloo-Lymington three-disc headcode, makes a welcome appearance on 21 July 1962. *St Lawrence* was previously shedded at Ashford and after the completion of the Kent Coast electrification scheme, made its way over to Nine Elms where it found employment for a short time, especially on seasonal workings such as these summer Lymington trains.

Left A mile or so out of Brockenhurst the branch to Lymington Pier diverges from the main line at Lymington Junction. On 19 August 1961 'M7' No 30480 is coasting round the curve from the branch to join the main line, with a push and pull train from Lymington Pier. The train is composed of a two-coach Urie 'Ironclad' set strengthened by a 100-seater compartment coach.

Right Prior to the arrival of the BR Standard tank locomotives, services on the Lymington branch were worked by Drummond 'M7' tanks, including No 30053. On 21 July 1962 it is heading away across the heathland towards Lymington Junction with a train from Lymington Pier. The train consists of an 'Ironclad' push and pull set strengthened by a Maunsell coach. After withdrawal and a stay in the United States, No 30053 is now owned by Drummond Locomotives Ltd and based on the Swanage Railway.

Below Not far from Lymington Junction the same day, No 30053 is working a push and pull train for Lymington Pier.

Left Lymington Town was the only intermediate station on the line to Lymington Pier. 'M7' No 30053 is about mid-way along the branch near Shirley Holms with a train for Brockenhurst on 21 July 1962

Above After a wet morning in the early summer of 1957, 'M7' No 30105 propels its train from Brockenhurst into Lymington Town, past the station's quite sizeable goods yard.

Left On the same day No 30105 is passing the signalbox as it leaves Lymington Town with a train for Brockenhurst. The sign on the signalbox directs motorists to the car ferry.

Right Surrounded by yachts moored in the harbour, 'M7' No 30053 slowly comes across the bridge over the Lymington River into the Town station on 21 July 1962.

Above After the withdrawal of the 'M7s', BR Standard tanks took over the branch workings. No 80134 is about to enter Lymington Town station, which was unusual in having a roof covering the single platform. No doubt such a facility would have been welcomed at this relatively exposed location when a gale was blowing up from the west.

Right 'Next Station For Boats' proclaims the notice under Lymington Town's station nameboard. On this wet day 'M7' No 30105 pauses at the station before leaving for the short run to the Pier station.

Lymington Junction to Bournemouth

Left The wide-open spaces of the New Forest gave plenty of scope for taking broadside pictures like this one of a rebuilt 'Merchant Navy'. The small wind-bent pine tree frames the locomotive as it crosses typical heathland between Lymington Junction and Sway.

Facing page Persistent rain is beginning to clear to the east as 'M7' No 30105 waits to leave Lymington Pier station for Brockenhurst on this dismal wet afternoon. Behind the diminutive Isle of Wight ferry on the right, there is a glimpse of the hills near Yarmouth.

Right Compared with the heavy traffic through the New Forest today, there seems to be little on the road as a rebuilt 'West Country' makes for Brockenhurst with an up train.

Left Towards the end of their career, the 'Lord Nelson' class was mainly employed on inter-regional workings, Southampton Docks boat trains and secondary services on the Bournemouth line, none of which really taxed them. With only a year to go before withdrawal, a sadly neglected looking No 30860 *Lord Hawke* is climbing away from Lymington Junction towards Sway with a down Saturdays Only (SO) summer working on 19 August 1961.

Right One of the Southern Region's smartly turned out BR Standard Class 4 2-6-0s No 76029 is working a down stopping service at the same location on the summer evening of Saturday 21 July 1962. This locomotive was allocated new to Eastleigh shed and spent the whole of its short 11 year life there.

Left Due to engineering work in connection with the electrification of the Bournemouth line, single line working is in operation at Sway. The signalman is handing over the token to the driver of rebuilt 'Battle of Britain' No 34088 to allow him to proceed towards Bournemouth.

Above On the approach to Christchurch, the Bournemouth line crosses over the river Avon by means of this girder bridge. A BR Standard Class 4MT 2-6-4T is rumbling over the structure with a train for Bournemouth.

Bournemouth

Above Holdenhurst Road bridge offered an excellent vantage point from which to photograph Bournemouth Central station with its imposing overall roof. Rebuilt 'Merchant Navy' No 35007 *Aberdeen Commonwealth* is making a smoky departure for Waterloo whilst one of the new 4VEP electric-units stands in the down platform. In the far distance a Crompton diesel-electric is at the head of the train and will take a portion of it on to Weymouth. This is a reminder that electrification of the line to Weymouth beyond Branksome was not brought into use until 1988.

Above The lengthy down platform at Bournemouth Central gave an unhindered view of the locomotive shed and was thus a popular place for locomotive-spotters and enthusiasts. The chalked graffiti on the wall is worth some study and clearly Gresley's 'A4' class has made an impression, perhaps inspired by the visit of No 4498 on a railtour from Waterloo.

Above Now that the BR Standard Class 5 4-6-0 No 73113 is about to disappear into the short tunnel under Holdenhurst Road, this group of lads at the end of the platform at Bournemouth Central station will be anticipating the next piece of steam action.

Above One of the footplate crew of BR Standard Class 4 2-6-0 No 76009 looks out of the cab to see what the Class 04 Drewry diesel is doing at the end of the up platform. I hope the two smartly dressed ladies don't get their new coats dirty standing by the very grubby 2-6-0.

Above A quiet moment between trains at the east end of the station – one of Bournemouth shed's BR Standard Class 4 2-6-4Ts No 80133 awaits its next turn of duty.

The 'Bournemouth Belle'

Right The up 'Belle' is waiting to leave Bournemouth Central station in 1966 when it was due away at 4.37pm. First Class Pullman Car *Ursula* which features in this picture, was built in 1928 and so far as I know still survives at the Spotgate Inn near Stone, Staffordshire as part of their restaurant. The sight of a passenger walking past *Ursula* carrying his bulging case is a reminder that surprisingly wheeled luggage was not generally available until the 1980s. Why hadn't someone thought of it earlier.

Near right A smartly dressed Pullman Car attendant stands ready to welcome passengers aboard as the train runs into the station.

Centre right '1960s chic observed'.

Far right More traditionally dressed passengers walk past Pullman Car No 64, also built in 1928, which is now based at the Bluebell Railway in Sussex. In the background others are waiting to join the train.

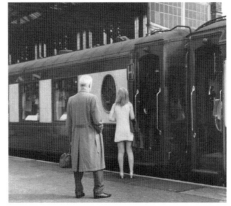

Bournemouth shed (71B)

Left On 3 June 1967, almost at the end of steam, 'A4' Gresley Pacific No 4498 *Sir Nigel Gresley* arrived at Bournemouth with an 'A4 Locomotive Society' special train from Waterloo. Here the unfamiliar outline of the locomotive is attracting much interest from the assembled spotters and enthusiasts.

Left Two enthusiasts on the down platform watch BR Standard Class 4 No 76026 moving out of the shed yard.

Above 'West Country' No 34023 *Blackmore Vale* was one of the last unrebuilt locomotives in service and was saved for preservation by the Bulleid Society. Here it is on the turntable at Bournemouth shed looking a little travel-worn but nevertheless nicely cleaned, perhaps hinting of immortality to come. Its nameplates have been removed for safe-keeping.

Above A view of the shed from the down platform in 1967 showing three different types of motive power – the old and the new. From the left, 4VEP electric-unit No 7702 painted in the rather attractive all-over blue livery, rebuilt 'Merchant Navy' No 35013 in the shed and Crompton Class 33 diesel-electric No D6520.

Below No 34060 is positioned ready for turning – note the visitors in the background on the right of the picture, in front of rebuilt 'Battle of Britain' No 34087. By this time, almost at the end of steam, the authorities tended to be rather more tolerant towards unofficial shed visits providing you kept well out of the way of moving locomotives.

Above A conveniently placed slab of concrete helps give this enthusiast a clear view of BR Standard Class 5 No 73118 being turned at the shed. This picture shows just how close large houses were, hence the need to keep smoke and noise in the yard to a minimum.

Above Amid the smoke and grime in front of the shed, a driver oils round Standard Class 5 No 73020 whilst rebuilt 'West Country' No 34093 *Saunton* awaits its next turn of duty.

Above A more unusual view of rebuilt 'West Country' No 34008 *Padstow* over the ash pit that emphasises the dirty conditions typical of the steam age.

Above The coaling facilities at Bournemouth shed were fairly primitive considering the number of locomotives it had to deal with – no large coaling tower here perhaps because of the proximity of residential housing, but simply the use of a crane and bucket. 'West Country' Pacific No 34023 has its tender topped up.

Above The overall roof at Bournemouth Central contributed to the impression of a large important station that of course it still is. Rebuilt 'West Country' No 34044 *Woolacombe* is coasting into the up platform thronged with passengers waiting to join the train for Waterloo. Happily the overall roof survives but the two middle tracks have been removed. The bookstall is open to the platform which was handy for the traveller who wanted to dash off the train to buy a newspaper or magazine.

Bournemouth to Poole

Left With the shed in the background, BR Standard Class 4 4-6-0 No 75076 leaves the station with a local train for Weymouth.

Above Bournemouth's pine trees, which gave their name to the famous 'Pines Express', feature in this picture of a BR Standard Class 4 4-6-0 as it approaches the Central station with a train from Weymouth.

Above On a local service from Weymouth, this BR Standard Class 4 is leaving Parkstone station on the sharp 1 in 60 climb towards Branksome.

Left Set amidst more whispering pine trees, Parkstone station was crossed by a rather ornate concrete bridge which can be seen in the background to this picture of BR Standard Class 5 No 73043 arriving with a stopping train to Weymouth.

Left All at sea – photographed across the choppy water of the large boating lake at Poole, this BR Standard Class 5 is on the causeway taking the line up towards Parkstone on a local train from Weymouth.

Right Travelling in the opposite direction, rebuilt 'Battle of Britain' No 34082 *615 Squadron* approaches Poole with a train for Weymouth.

Left Rebuilt 'West Country' No 34098 *Templecombe* has arrived at Poole's sharply curved platform with a train from Weymouth. The old station buildings seen in this picture have now been replaced and the curve straightened out as part of the comprehensive redevelopment of the station and the surrounding roads.

Below A survivor at Poole station, dating from Southern Railway days though now looking rather corroded no doubt due to the salty air off the nearby sea.

Facing page On this wet dismal day in 1958 'West Country' No 34040 *Crewkerne*, working a train for the Ringwood loop and Brockenhurst, is coming over the level crossing that was located on the Bournemouth side of Poole station. This crossing has long since been replaced by a bridge as part of the redevelopment of Poole town centre. No 34040 was rebuilt in October 1960 and went on to last until the end of steam on the Bournemouth line.

The Ringwood loop

Left 'M7' No 30031 is pulling away from Holmsley with a train for Brockenhurst on 21 July 1962. Local services on the Ringwood loop from Brockenhurst to Broadstone and on through Poole to Bournemouth West or Central were comparatively sparse, a typical end to end journey taking around 1¼ hours. The Ringwood loop closed on 4 May 1964 and Holmsley station is now a restaurant and tearoom.

Right Through luck, I am just in the right position to photograph BR Standard Class 4 No 76056, probably on a train for Salisbury, about to pass Bournemouth-bound 'M7' No 30129 on the outskirts of Ringwood.

Left On summer Saturdays some trains were diverted via the Ringwood loop to take pressure off the main line via Christchurch. On a hot 21 July 1962 near Wimborne, this east-bound working, possibly originating at Swanage, is hauled by rebuilt 'West Country' No 34095 *Brentor*.

Right Preparing to leave Broadstone, 'West Country' No 34011 *Tavistock* has come round the Ringwood loop with the 9.15am Saturdays Only through train from Waterloo to Swanage and has crossed to the line for Hamworthy Junction. On Nine Elms duty No 44, *Tavistock* will come off the train at Wogret Junction and another locomotive will work it down the branch to Swanage. Meanwhile No 34011 will run light engine to Bournemouth shed.

Above 'M7' No 30028 is sandwiched between a luggage van and a Urie 'Ironclad' push and pull set on this train for Brockenhurst, which has just left Ringwood. It looks as if the down line has recently been re-laid judging by the new ballast and the speed restriction sign in the cess.

Above On the approach to Broadstone, one of the useful 'Q' class 0-6-0s No 30535 is in charge of a train from Salisbury, unusually formed of an old push and pull set leading three Bulleid coaches. The line to Salisbury branched off the Ringwood loop at Alderbury Junction near West Moors. It only had a sparse service of some five trains a day each way, and closed on 4 May 1964.

Bournemouth West, Broadstone and the Somerset & Dorset line

Above In contrast to bustling Bournemouth Central station, Bournemouth West was comparatively quiet in comparison but offered the chance to see interesting Somerset & Dorset line trains as well as local services, like this one to Salisbury hauled by 'T9' No 30313. The train will shortly leave on its 38¼-mile journey that will take about 1½ hours. The station closed in October 1965.

Above Later at Broadstone station, the wheezy old 'T9' is starting out of the station for its run through quiet countryside to Salisbury via Daggons Road and Downton.

Above On a journey to Weymouth who could resist a chance to see the scenic Somerset & Dorset line which ran in a south east/north west direction through Wessex from Broadstone to Bath. At Broadstone, where the Somerset & Dorset line met the Ringwood loop, Bath Green Park allocated Standard Class 4 4-6-0 No 75071 is entering the station with a southbound train bound for Bournemouth West, composed of Southern Region stock.

Left BR Standard Class 5 No 73049 has just left Broadstone station with a local train from the Somerset & Dorset and is starting the descent of the 1 in 75 bank towards Poole. The line on the left of the picture leads to Hamworthy Junction.

Left Some 17 miles from Broadstone, Bournemouth shed's rebuilt 'West Country' No 34045 *Ottery St. Mary* is slowly passing Shillingstone station with the southbound 'Pines Express' on Saturday 19 August 1961 – the train was due to call at Blandford Forum at 5.20pm five miles further on. Although Shillingstone station closed in March 1966, it is currently undergoing extensive restoration under the Shillingstone Railway Project.

Right Further north on a fine summer Saturday in 1962, this powerful combination of Standard Class 4 4-6-0 No 75027 and rebuilt 'West Country' No 34044 *Woolacombe,* make an impressive sight between Chilcompton and Binegar with a train for Bournemouth West.

Left Standard Class 9F 2-10-0s Nos 92203 and 92220 were destined to survive after the end of steam working on British Railways. No 92220 *Evening Star,* seen here crossing Prestleigh viaduct in 1963 with a train for Bath, already had its place in history as the last British Railways steam locomotive to be built.

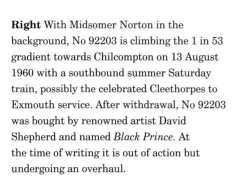

Right With Midsomer Norton in the background, No 92203 is climbing the 1 in 53 gradient towards Chilcompton on 13 August 1960 with a southbound summer Saturday train, possibly the celebrated Cleethorpes to Exmouth service. After withdrawal, No 92203 was bought by renowned artist David Shepherd and named *Black Prince*. At the time of writing it is out of action but undergoing an overhaul.

Above left Ancient and modern – near Shoscombe and Single Hill Halt, an unidentified BR Standard Class 4 and one of the S&D line's elderly 4F 0-6-0s, head south with a summer Saturday extra on 28 July 1962. Another 10 miles or so of climbing is ahead of the locomotives before they reach Masbury summit.

Left In the other direction, with the climb over the Mendip hills over, S&D 2-8-0 No 53807 coasts downhill near Shoscombe and Single Hill Halt in August 1962 with a northbound train, which includes a Southern Region Maunsell brake coach next to the locomotive.

Above With only some 11 miles to run to Broadstone where the S&D will join the Ringwood loop, Bath Green Park BR Standard Class 5 No 73051 piloting rebuilt 'West Country' No 34028 *Eddystone* have just left Blandford Forum with this lengthy train for Bournemouth in 1959.

Hamworthy

Left Hamworthy Junction was the starting point for the branch to Poole Quay as well as the direct line to Brockenhurst via Broadstone and Ringwood. Here BR Standard Class 4 No 75069 is leaving the station with a lightweight two-coach local train to Weymouth.

Below Sister locomotive No 75075 is pulling away from Hamworthy Junction station, past its extensive carriage sidings, with a train for Weymouth. In the background a Bulleid Pacific is at the head of some blue and grey painted stock forming an inter-regional service starting from Poole, which has been berthed on the Poole Quay branch.

Left Between Hamworthy and Poole the line comes round a long sweeping curve on a causeway across Holes Bay, constructed when the direct line from Bournemouth was built. Even today this is still a popular and attractive location for photography. Set off by a picturesque pine tree bent inwards by the prevailing wind off the sea, an unidentified BR Standard Class 4 2-6-4T is on the approach to Poole with this train from Weymouth.

The Swanage branch

Right What a difference a thorough clean would have made to this rather neglected looking rebuilt 'Merchant Navy' No 35008 *Orient Line,* but at least it still retains its nameplates. Mail is waiting to be loaded on to the Waterloo bound service which is drawing to a stop at Wareham station, where there will be a Swanage branch connection.

Below On summer Saturdays there were through trains to and from Swanage as depicted on page 122. In the summer of 1962 the 9.20am train from the seaside resort, complete with restaurant car, ran to Bournemouth Central, and thence non-stop to Waterloo where it arrived at 12.39pm, a journey time of a creditable 3 hours 19 minutes. Here is a through train from Waterloo to Swanage, hauled by rebuilt 'Battle of Britain' No 34062 *17 Squadron* which is lifting its 10 coaches up the 1 in 80 gradient out of Corfe Castle at Townsend bridge.

Right This is one of the enduring vistas that can still be enjoyed on the Swanage branch. I am standing by the A351 road at Afflington bridge to photograph this 'M7' coasting down the gradient towards Corfe Castle with a push and pull train for Wareham.

Left 'M7' No 30108 is near Norden with a train from Swanage. Behind the train is the by then disused gated Eldon's Siding and the connection with the Fayle & Co narrow gauge clay tramway.

Left Consecutively numbered 'M7s' Nos 30107 and 30108 pass at Corfe Castle station with trains for Wareham and Swanage respectively. This scene looks very similar today, though the once long demolished signalbox on the down side has been reinstated and a footbridge installed by the Swanage Railway.

Right Another summer Saturday picture taken in 1961 shows the stock of a through train to Swanage returning empty from the resort. 'M7' No 30107 is piloting rebuilt 'West Country' No 34093 *Saunton* near Afflington bridge. The Pacific is too long to use the turntable at Swanage so is having to return to Bournemouth shed tender first.

Right Here is the compact terminus station at Swanage in 1962 still retaining its goods yard. 'M7' No 30108 is leaving the bay platform with a train for Wareham.

Wareham to Dorchester

Left Nowadays is not possible to take pictures at this location since the growth of trees and bushes prevents a clear view of the line where it crosses the river Piddle or Trent just to the west of Wareham. Alison and Richard are waving to the driver of rebuilt 'Battle of Britain' No 34082 *615 Squadron* which is working a Waterloo to Weymouth train – their red jackets add a bright splash of colour on this rather overcast day.

Right At East Stoke to the west of Wogret Junction, the line ran alongside the river Frome. On a summer evening as the sun moved round to the west some lovely 'glint' pictures could be taken, such as this Weymouth bound train hauled by a rebuilt 'West Country' No 34040 *Crewkerne*.

Right Rebuilt 'West Country' No 34024 which has lost its nameplates, has just passed the little level crossing at East Stoke with a train for Weymouth. In the foreground the River Frome flows serenely towards the sea at Poole Harbour and behind the trees on the left of the picture is St Mary's church.

Right Between Wool and Moreton the nature of the country changes as the line climbs out of the valley of the river Frome across Winfrith Heath. I am standing on the heath facing west and have been lucky enough to photograph two trains passing, one hauled by a BR Standard 4 '76000' class 2-6-0.

Left Looking in the opposite direction this picture conveys something more of the atmosphere of Winfrith Heath. A BR Standard Class 4 2-6-0 is working a typical local Bournemouth to Weymouth line service.

Above Rebuilt 'West Country' No 34004 is coming over the level crossing at Wool station with an up train from Weymouth, which includes some blue and white liveried BR Mk 1 coaches in its formation. This level crossing on the busy A352 main road to Dorchester continues to cause some traffic congestion especially at peak times.

Above Set off by the neat signalbox, level crossing gates and vintage station nameboard, an unidentified BR Standard Class 5 is entering the small station at Moreton with a Weymouth train, The village of Moreton is more than a mile away to the north in the valley of the river Frome.

Right Meanwhile in the opposite direction and set against a stormy sky, rebuilt 'Battle of Britain' No 34077 *603 Squadron* is arriving at the station with an up train from Weymouth. Despite its unkempt external condition the Pacific makes a fine sight lit by a shaft of low evening sun.

Right Before the provision of a new up platform at Dorchester South in 1970, eastbound trains were obliged to reverse into the original station platform, which dated from the time when the line was planned to be extended towards Exeter. Rebuilt 'West Country' No 34047 *Callington* has completed this movement and is now pulling out with its three-coach train bound for Bournemouth.

Right In the opposite direction BR Standard Class 4 2-6-0 No 76009 is departing with a vans train bound for Weymouth. In the left background some wagons can be seen parked opposite the up platform and beyond that the imposing buildings of the Eldridge Pope Dorchester Brewery.

Dorchester to Yeovil line

Left Almost to the end of steam on the Southern Region, trains of perishable Channel Islands produce, usually hauled by rebuilt Bulleid Pacifics, could be photographed on the Western Region line to Yeovil and Westbury. Rebuilt 'Battle of Britain' No 34060 passes the attractive little station at Maiden Newton with one of these workings. On the right hand side of the station is the overall roofed bay platform for the Bridport branch trains. The branch closed in 1975.

Right Here rebuilt 'West Country' No 34013 from Salisbury shed is working another northbound train of Channel Islands produce near Evershot.

Dorchester to Weymouth

Facing page After the Southern Region line joins the former Great Western route at Dorchester Junction, there is a gradient of 1 in 91 towards Bincombe tunnel. I am standing on the east side of the line to photograph a BR Standard Class 4 4-6-0 hauled freight train, silhouetted against the sky on the high embankment, as it makes its way towards Weymouth.

Left On this fine summer day in July 1965, rebuilt 'West Country' No 34004 *Yeovil* is emerging from the north portal of the 819 yards long Bincombe tunnel with a train for Bournemouth and Waterloo. Adjacent to the neat little platelayers hut, the entrance to the tunnel is guarded by a Great Western Railway lower quadrant signal.

Right A BR Standard '76000' Class 4 2-6-0 working a local train for Bournemouth, has come through the 48 yards long south tunnel at Bincombe. In sharp contrast to the steep sides of the cutting at the Dorchester end of the main tunnel, there are signs of slippage here perhaps because of local instability in the strata.

Left This is the view from above Bincombe tunnel looking towards Dorchester. In place of the more usual '76000' Class 4 2-6-0, Ivatt 2-6-2T No 41298 is on this local service for Weymouth which is passing Bincombe tunnel signalbox. Where a banking locomotive was used to assist an up train, it could drop off here and cross over to return back to Weymouth.

Left In general double heading on the Southern Region was not common but probably most often seen on the steep six miles or so climb out of Weymouth. However a banking locomotive would more usually be employed to save the time needed to detach the assisting locomotive. Here 'Battle of Britain' No 34065 *Hurricane* is piloting a rebuilt 'West Country' Pacific out of the south tunnel at Bincombe with the 5.35pm train from Weymouth to Waterloo in 1959.

Above I am standing on the embankment above the by then closed but charmingly named Upwey Wishing Well Halt which saw its last passengers in 1957. This 11-coach train plus a van is being worked up the 1 in 50 gradient out of Weymouth by 'West Country' No 34041 *Wilton,* banked in the rear by a BR Standard Class 4 4-6-0. Today this location is still popular for photographing steam specials, though the embankment is now largely obscured by the growth of trees. A new bypass road has been built into Weymouth, which together with the spread of new housing around Upwey, has irrecoverably altered this fine rural vista.

Above As No 34041 passed me I have been able to capture this unusual view of it about to enter the first of the two tunnels at Bincombe.

Right On a fine summer evening in 1966, buttercups and a solitary horse in the meadow adjacent to Upwey & Broadwey station set off this picture of rebuilt 'Merchant Navy' No 35030 leaving the station with an up train.

Right In July 1965, BR Standard Class 4 No 76057 is pulling out of Upwey & Broadwey station. Sadly it displays the typical external condition of many locomotives on the Bournemouth line towards the end of steam. In the foreground is the platform face of the one time Abbotsbury branch. The GWR sign at the platform end instructs all up goods and mineral trains to stop dead in view of the steep 1 in 74 gradient down to Weymouth which lay ahead. No 76057's glory days were in the latter half of the 1950s when it was allocated to Redhill. There it would have been used on heavy inter-regional trains over the line to Reading or south towards Brighton.

Above Watched by two elderly residents, who are standing close to where the branch line to Abbotsbury used to run, BR Standard Class 5 No 73022 is passing the signalbox at Upwey & Broadwey station with the Channel Islands boat train bound for Waterloo in July 1965.

Right 'King Arthur' 4-6-0 No 30772 *Sir Percivale* is approaching Upwey & Broadwey station in March 1958 with an up goods train. The 'King Arthurs' had all gone by the end of 1962, most of their workings being taken over by the new BR Standard classes.

Right The heavy Channel Islands boat train that left Weymouth in the mid afternoon was banked out of Weymouth by whatever suitable locomotive that might be available. In this case a BR Standard Class 5 4-6-0 is used and is approaching Upwey & Broadwey station in July 1965. Assistance for a train of 10 coaches or over was usual, but mandatory for 12 coaches or more.

Left On this idyllic early spring afternoon in 1964, rebuilt 'West Country' No 34037 *Clovelly* is pulling away from Upwey & Broadwey station on the last stage of its journey to Weymouth. The catch points in the middle distance mark the location of the divergence of the branch to Abbotsbury. Although the branch closed to passengers in 1952, it remained open for goods traffic to the first station Upwey until 1962. In the distance the main line curves round through the station towards the south Dorset Downs which dominate the landscape.

Facing page top left Close to Radipole Halt, a bridge on the A354 road to Dorchester crossed the main line and offered an excellent vantage point from which to photograph northbound workings. Here one evening in early spring, BR Standard Class 5 No 73020 is piloting rebuilt 'West Country' No 34047 *Callington* as they forge out of Weymouth with a heavy train,

Facing page bottom left An unidentified Bulleid Pacific is approaching the simply constructed Radipole Halt serving Radipole Lake (now a nature reserve) and the village. It was situated a mile or so out of Weymouth and survived until early 1984 when it was officially closed, having seen its last passengers at the end of 1983.

Weymouth Shed (70G)

Facing page right A driver and his fireman have a chat at Weymouth shed before boarding rebuilt 'West Country' No 34036 *Westward Ho* that is being prepared to work the afternoon Channel Islands boat train to Waterloo.

Right A little later No 34036 is almost ready to leave the shed that was situated on the east side of the line about a 20 minute walk from the station. Access was by way of a cinder path through some allotments.

Above Driver Peter Miller, originally a GWR man, is checking round Weymouth-based BR Standard Class 5 No 73018 before working a local train to Bournemouth.

Above Weymouth was a GWR shed coded 82F in BR Western Region days. However on transfer to the Southern Region in 1958 it became 71G, then finally 70G at the end of steam. Unlike other Southern Region sheds such as Nine Elms, Weymouth's coaling facilities were not the most advanced as can be seen from this picture of rebuilt 'Merchant Navy' No 35028 *Clan Line* having its tender topped up from coal hoppers which had to be filled by hand.

Left The crew of rebuilt 'West Country' No 34034 *Honiton* have balanced their locomotive on the turntable and are starting to push it round.

Above The GWR designed 65ft turntable at Weymouth shed, situated at the north end of the yard, has just been used to turn rebuilt 'Merchant Navy' No 35028 *Clan Line*.

Right This is a view from the coaling stage of the spacious shed yard at Weymouth – a BR Standard Class 4 has just left the station for Bournemouth whilst outside the shed rebuilt 'West Country' No 34001 and a BR Standard Class 5 await their next turns of duty.

Below Down at the seaside terminus in early 1958, a reminder of the Great Western Railway origins of Weymouth is provided by the Western Region pannier tank, No 4624, on station pilot duties. On the right BR Standard Class 5 No 73117 waits to leave for Bournemouth. The station was rebuilt in the mid 1980s and is now much reduced in size.

Above In total contrast to the imposing entrance to Waterloo depicted at the beginning of this book, here is the end of the line at Weymouth station 142¾ miles from the capital. BR Standard Class 4 No 76010, standing at the buffer stop, is seen from adjacent Queen Street.

Left Between Weymouth and Radipole Halt a small bridge crossed the line that was well suited for photographing trains leaving the seaside station, as well as giving a good view of the shed area. Rebuilt 'Merchant Navy' No 35013 *Blue Funnel* on a train for Waterloo, is passing the sidings which led to the Weymouth Quay line, used by the Channel Islands boat trains.

Right Though the final destination of trains from Waterloo, Weymouth was not the end of the line, since apart from the branch to the Quay used by the Channel Islands boat trains, the other branch to Portland and Easton on the Isle of Portland remained open for goods traffic until 1962. On a delightfully warm spring day in March 1958, pannier tank No 8799 from Weymouth shed has just arrived at Portland, with a freight working from Easton that includes three wagons containing blocks of Portland stone. Behind the train loom the heights of the Isle of Portland and to the left, houses for personnel from the big naval base.

Vale Vapor! – Rebuilt Bulleid Pacific No 34001 *Exeter* heads out of Weymouth as the day draws to an end.